The
Misericc
of
Norwich Cathedral

by Martial Rose

Photographs by Ken Harvey

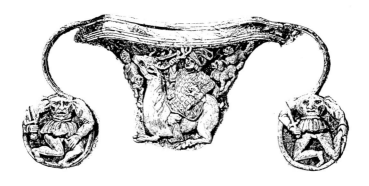

The Larks Press

ACKNOWLEDGEMENTS

Our preliminary study of the misericords of Norwich Cathedral was supported by the Dean and Chapter. We received great assistance from the Sacrist, George Allison, and his staff, and also from Jean Vincent and James Page. To all we express our thanks. We are particularly grateful for the enthusiasm and encouragement given to our work by Canon Michael McLean.

Published by The Larks Press
Ordnance Farmhouse, Guist Bottom, Dereham
Norfolk NR20 5PF
01328 829207
email: Larks.Press@btinternet.com
Website: www.booksatlarkspress.co.uk

First published in larger format in November 1994
ISBN 0 948400 25 0

This edition published September 2003

Printed by the Lanceni Press
Garrood Drive, Fakenham
01328 851578

British Library Cataloguing-in-Publication Data
A catalogue record for this book is available from the British Library.

ISBN 1 904006 15 9

What is a Misericord?

The word misericord is derived from the Latin *misericordia* which means mercy. A misericord is the ledge supported by a corbel on the underside of a choir-stall which is only to be seen when the seat is in a tipped-up position. In early times this ledge was provided as a rest especially for the frail and aged monks in an endeavour to ease the physical strain of standing through the eight or nine services which they were required to attend during the course of each twenty-four hours. The daily offices, starting in the very early hours, were Matins, Lauds, Prime, Terce, Sext, Nones, Vespers, and Compline; added to which the monks were expected to attend at least one Mass each day.

Although wooden choir-stalls might have been set up in some English churches by the 10th century, they probably provided places for standing rather than seats. Seats were introduced in the 12th century. Rochester and Salisbury can furnish us with examples of seats with misericords in the 13th century. The enclosure of the choir-stalls with protective high backs, broad canopies above, deep seats, and solid desks in front, must have provided a welcome shelter from the cold and nipping draughts that swept through those lofty, large, unheated monasteries and cathedrals. The merciful addition of misericords must have eased considerably the rigours of the monks' daily life.

Brief History of the Choir-Stalls

From the 12th century onwards a succession of fires and natural disasters led to fundamental changes in the structure and furnishing of Norwich Cathedral. For instance the former wooden roofing was replaced by stone vaulting, and the earlier arrangement of the choir was completely superseded by the choir-stalls of the 15th and early 16th centuries. It is thought that the 14th century stalls suffered in the seven-day storm in 1361 (8) in which the cathedral tower was blown down and the choir seriously damaged. It is probable that the plans that were put in hand for refurbishing the stalls were not implemented until the second decade of the 15th century. From the great number of armorial shields that appear as supporters and elbow-rests among the stalls that were put in place during Wakering's episcopate (1416-25) it can be deduced that a number of East Anglian gentry, many bound together by ties of blood, underwrote the construction of a complete set of choir furniture. Some of these patrons died towards the end of the 14th century, (John Le Strange in 1375, William de Ufford in 1382, Sir William Wingfield in 1378) and many died at the time of the battle of Harfleur in 1415 (Sir Thomas Morley, Sir Robert Berney, and Michael de la Pole, the second Earl of Suffolk). A key factor in helping to date the Wakering stalls is the misericord S6 which depicts Richard Courtenay, Bishop of Norwich from 1413-15.

(Numbers in the text refer to the numbered book list at the back of the book.)

He accompanied King Henry V to Harfleur where, like the Earl of Suffolk, he died of dysentery. This misericord is said to be the only one in England in which a bishop is positively identified. Courtenay's initials R and C appear beneath a crown, for he claimed kinship with the king (8). These initials are carved, one either side, beneath the ledge. It was customary for knights before setting off for battle to make bequests, in the event of their death, to holy places. It is most probable that the building of the new choir came about through the personal involvement and contribution of a number of East Anglian families, and that it was the additional funds raised after the battles of Harfleur and Agincourt in 1415 that finally launched the building programme.

The early 15th century choir-stalls, together with their desks and tall canopies, extended from the present choir and, at the same level, filled the space between the transept arches of the crossing. Lightning struck the roof of the nave in 1463 and the ensuing fire not only destroyed the roof but also affected many other parts of the cathedral. Many of the choir-stalls were damaged. Repairs were undertaken in Bishop Goldwell's episcopate (1472-99): some seating was rearranged, some new misericords were carved, and new canopies were built which extended across the transepts and over the first three stalls on either side at the east end of the present choir. The fire of 1509, which started in the roof of one of the transepts, caused further damage to the choir-stalls in the crossing. Repairs to the stalls and a further rearrangement of the seating were undertaken during Bishop Nykke's episcopate, 1501-36. The canopies in the crossing were removed in 1851, and there the Goldwell stalls were lowered and for the first time access given to the crossing from the transepts for congregational use. To improve access further, in 1948 six stalls were removed: four were placed in the south of the sanctuary, with the function of sedilia, and two were moved to the north side of the sanctuary. The reorganization of the choir seating in 1948 has left us with a legacy of 64 choir- stalls.

The Number and Placement of the Choir-Stalls

The original choir most probably contained 70 stalls. Roman numerals which have been marked on the back of the seats confirm this figure, a readily acceptable canonical number. Christ sent 70 disciples out into the world (Luke 10. 1-20). The monks of course were not being appointed to go out into the world, indeed Chaucer and Langland criticised them for their being too secular. But 70 was an accepted figure for a closed community. When William of Wykeham founded Winchester College in 1382, the charter made provision for 70 poor scholars. And when, at the end of the 14th and the beginning of 15th century, plans were laid for the building of a new choir at Norwich, provision was made for 70 stalls.

The 70 stalls were allotted as follows: the bishop, the prior, the sub-prior, the sacrist, precentor, chancellor, the four archdeacons, and 60 monks. The bishop's seat was the first return stall on the south side, and the prior took the first return stall on the north side. The sub-prior and the four archdeacons sat in the next senior seats in the return stalls and those adjoining. The precentor took the stall just west of the crossing on the south side, and the chancellor took the stall opposite the precentor on the north side. When first the stalls were put in place, or on the occasion of rebuilding, there is some probability that the occupants of the seats had the opportunity of suggesting the subject of their misericord before it was carved.

Of the remaining 64 choir-stalls no misericords appear in the following stalls: S1, S19, N1, and N2. The misericord carved for N19 is in a style completely different from any of the others and might, as Whittingham suggests, have come from elsewhere in the cathedral, perhaps the Lady Chapel. Of the 59 remaining misericords 22 we might characterize as Wakering's, 35 as Goldwell's, and 2 as Nykke's.

Wakering's misericords are to be distinguished by the shape of the misericord ledge, the edge of which is carved in six concave curves. A ribbing runs round the edge. Also among these misericords and elbow-rests there is ample evidence of the patronage afforded by local gentry in securing the rebuilding of the choir: coats of arms abound as well as some delicate portrayal of the gentry themselves, for instance Sir William Clere of Ormesby and his wife (S4), Bishop Courtenay (S6), and Sir Robert de Illey (N4). The Wakering seats are also marked at shoulder level along the back-rest with a battlemented pattern.

The ledges of Goldwell's misericords are rounded and comprise two lobes, sometimes edged with a thick rib, sometimes without. The two Nykke misericords, post 1509 (S26 and S29), are characterized by the carvings on the edge of the seat. Spaced at intervals is a diamond set into a square. The anomaly, however, about these Nykke misericords is that the ledge itself resembles the Wakering form, and the style of carving also reflects that of Wakering's period. A possibility is that these two stalls were reworked from earlier damaged material.

Style and Composition

The composition of most misericords is fairly uniform: a central subject with supporters left and right. Very often the supporters are entirely unrelated to the central subject. Norwich Cathedral has an above average number of supporters that relate to the central carving. Examples would be the mermaid suckling a lion, with the dolphins as supporters (N9), Bishop Courtenay with supporting scenes of his role as pastor and educationist (S6), and the Deadly Sin of Lechery supported by the unregenerate anthropophagi (S30).

Dramatic play is made by the carver of the curved space between the underside of the ledge and the flat base of the misericord. The pressure of the overhang presses down upon Gluttony (N18) whose head is tipped back under the ledge as he empties his tankard, and his hat falls off the back of his head. Another example is that in which Anger, another Deadly Sin, has his head forced down by the curve on the right, while on the left the boar, on which he rides, thrusts up its snout and tusks into the overhanging ledge (N16).

There is a change of style between the early and late fifteenth century work. The earlier work, whether representing repose (N7) or conflict (S2), is characterized by simplicity with the carving of a single figure, or of two figures interacting: the hunter (N5) or the mermaid feeding the lion (N9) or St George overcoming the dragon (S8). The later work tends to portray more intricate story material such as the farmyard scene (S27) or the apes and their wheelbarrow (N27) or the teacher spanking his pupil (S25). The representation of coats of arms is restricted to the earlier period.

Among the most attractive carvings are the elbow-rests which often present us with masterpieces in miniature. Again, the use of the natural curve of the rest to accommodate the sideways and downwards flow of curling hair, angels' wings, an eagle's twisted neck, or the acrobat's back-flip is often exquisite.

Range of Subjects

We have become accustomed, particularly at Norwich, to seeing the operation of a grand scheme when choice of subject has to inform a major architectural development. The roof bosses in the vaulting are an obvious example, but the same care would have obtained in the consideration of subjects for stained glass, for reredoses, and for murals. In such choice of subject integrity of scheme and propriety of place would have been guiding principles. The sculpture figures in the niches of the Erpingham Gate exemplify further the care taken in following such principles. Yet such care did not obtain for the misericord carvings in Norwich or elswhere. The subjects chosen seem to have been picked at random. The choice ranges over a great variety of beasts, real and imaginary, seasonal tasks, country games, domestic squabbles, kings, queens, knights and their ladies, woodwose men, Green Men, allegorical representations of the Seven Deadly Sins, and representations from classical or Arthurian stories. Most interestingly, the representation of Old or New Testament comprises an emphatic minority of msericord subject-matter. Why should this be, within the very centre of church, monastery, or cathedral? Some writers suggest that this is because it was thought unseemly that carvings of holy subjects should be sat upon by so base a part of the human anatomy. This, I believe, is quite untenable. It so happens that some of the most accomplished carvings of holy subjects are expressly placed in the stalls of some of the most senior clerics. The carving of the Resurrecton in the Dean's stall at Lincoln Minster is a case in point, and also the crowning of the Virgin Mary in the Archdeacon's stall (N3) in Norwich. During the Middle Ages the misericords would not have found a much wider viewing circle than the monks themselves, and those who were not sitting on a carving directly derived from the Bible were most likely to have as a misericord a subject that drew attention, in an allegorical form, to the follies and pitfalls of this life.

The medley of subjects offered by the 60 misericords in Norwich Cathedral does not conform to any clear categorization, but the following groups are at least discernible:

1. Where it is apparent from the heraldic symbols that a stall has been paid for by a donor the subject is usually that of a knight, or a knight and his lady, or St George.

In the case of Isabella Beauchamp of Warwick, who became a nun, the subject is that of the Coronation of the Virgin (N3).

2. The Coronation of the Virgin is one of very few on a biblical or apochryphal theme. Others would be Samson's struggle with the lion (N13), and the owls (S21, and N17) representing the blindness of the Synagogue. In addition there are the symbols of the Evangelists: the angel of St Matthew (S15), the lion of St Mark (S23), and the ox of St Luke (S24). Another Apocalypse reference is St Michael slaying the seven-headed dragon (N11).

3. The portraits, apart from those of the donors, represent Bishop Courtenay (S6), probably Bishop Goldwell (N20), and perhaps King Henry IV (S12).

4. The Seven Deadly Sins are represented by Lechery (S30), Anger (N16), Gluttony (N18), and by Avarice, carved as an elbow-rest (N26 Right). I doubt whether, as Whittingham indicates, Sloth (S27) is represented.

5. Two signs of the Zodiac are carved, Taurus (S26) and Leo (S29), the Bull and the Lion. Both are dated after the 1509 fire.

6. There is a plethora of carvings of wyverns, dragons, eagles, hawks, pelicans, griffins, dogs, pigs, apes, lions and boars. According to the bestiaries each animal has his own allegorical meaning.

7. The two Green Men (S20 and N24).

8. The woodwose or wild men (S7, S11, S28, N31).

Were the Misericords painted?

It is unclear whether the misericords would originally have been painted. It would seem that the superstructures of choir-stalls in England were painted in the Middle Ages, and traces of gold leaf are still to be seen on some stalls in Peterborough Cathedral (19). In Norwich Cathedral, where so many heraldic shields have been carved among the misericords, the probability that these shields would have declared their heraldic colours is high. Whittingham is categorical in his belief that the stalls were painted, but the evidence he puts forward is less than convincing: 'The blank scrolls on the Evangelists prove that the stalls were originally painted'. (23) There was certainly painting of the stalls and the misericords in post-Reformation times. Following the decrees in 1547 in the reign of Edward VI against the superstitious veneration of relics and images, some of the images, instead of being destroyed were painted over with whitewash. Further coats of whitewash might well have been applied during the succeeding centuries We read in a letter of 1846 from John Adey Repton to Sir William Ellis: 'We thank the Dean and Chapter (of Norwich) for the good taste which has restored the old dark oak in the stalls of the choir, which was before covered with white paint.'(15)

Conclusion

It is clear that the carving of the cycle of roof bosses set into the nave vaulting in the third quarter of the 15th century followed a precise instruction from the cathedral's authorities. The work was patterned, deliberate, and followed the story of the Creation of the World to the Last Judgement. It paralleled the substance of the contemporary mystery plays. The misericords, completed mostly during the same century, would appear to have been carved with no overall direction, no unifying scheme, and with sparse reference to the Scriptures. Yet however haphazard the placing of the carvings seems to have been, as one passes through the threatening forests of dragons, wyverns, lions, griffins, and other predatory creatures, the atmosphere comes to resemble that, not of the mystery plays, but of the medieval morality plays. Struggling against the monsters, which symbolize the forces of evil, are the wild men, the men of nature, seeking to tame the beasts, the warrior contends with the griffin, the lions are confronted by two stalwart fighters, St George overcomes the dragon, and St Michael slays the beast with seven heads. Gluttony, Pride, Anger, and Avarice are shown as distortions of the human spirit; and the many elbow-rests, which show fashionably-dressed men of authority, and soldiers wearing their armour, in the jaws of hell, recall the impending judgement that suddenly confonts Everyman. The monks fingering these elbow-rests in the course of their offices would have pondered on the grinding power of those teeth. The misericord carvers mostly took their inspiration from illuminated manuscripts. Their monsters perhaps were taken from bestiaries or the marginalia of psalters. The scenes of wrestling, or of a fox running off with a goose, or a teacher spanking a recalcitrant pupil might equally have been taken from such marginalia. But such scenes are from life and not from fantasy, and the vitality of the work impresses on one the carver's familiarity with the detail of such scenes.

The religious fervour of the Reformation and in particular the puritanical extremism of the Cromwellian period in the 17th century have deprived us of uncountable treasures that were cherished in our churches. Misericords, however, have been left relatively unharmed. Certainly some of the misericords carrying overt Christian imagery have been destroyed or partly destroyed, but because such imagery was not a main feature of the work, the vandals have left a great many marvellous carvings unscathed. Norwich Cathedral is extraordinarily fortunate to have retained 60 of its misericords most of which are not only in very good condition but can be ranked among the finest work in this genre throughout the country. The men who undertook the carving in the 15th century were given scope of choice and freedom of execution. A spirit of joy and freedom informs these carvings with zest and vitality. Happy the viewer who catches a small part of that infectious spirit!

Misericords on the south side of the choir, transept and sanctuary

S1

A misericord representing Maundy Thursday – Christ washing the feet of the disciples. Not illustrated. (Installed in 2001)

Elbow-rests

Right: The head of a bishop. He wears a mitre from which wavy hair descends on each side. Foliage is carved behind the hair. This first return stall on the south side in pre-Reformation times would have been reserved for the bishop of the diocese.

Left: A much damaged angel.

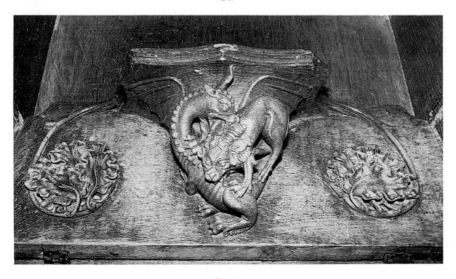

Centre

A dragon with spread wings fights with a lion. They bite each other's backs. The lion's fore-claws are thrust into the dragon's neck. One of its ears has broken off. The dragon has a single horn in the middle of its forehead. It is a four-footed beast and its fore-feet are seen on the extreme left of the carving. The curled dragon's tail has snapped off. A beaded ridge runs from the dragon's forehead to its tail. The dragon fighting with the lion symbolizes the forces of evil against those of good. Such a struggle is witnessed by the Arthurian knight, Ivain, in the romance told by Chrétien de Troyes (see N23).

Supporters

Both Left and Right are of oak leaves. On the Left side are also a few acorns.

Elbow-rests

Right: As for S1 Left.
Left: An angel with his arms broken off. He wears an amice and a tunicle with a feathered border above a pleated alb. A crown is in front of him which no doubt he would have been holding with his hands. His wings sweep downward on either side. The angel's hair flows out horizontally behind him. A hawk is in flight on each side. Hawks, one of the heraldic motifs which helps to identify and date much of the choir-stall carving, are associated in the choir with Bishop Wakering (1416-25).

Centre

A pattern of intertwining branches supports seven roses and two rose-buds. Whittingham describes the carving as a bush of Lancastrian roses. A similar carving appears in a south return stall misericord in St Margaret's, Kings Lynn, in precisely the same position (S3).

Supporters

A large rose features both Left and Right. It has the same design as the centre roses but is four times as large.

Elbow Rests

Right: As for S2 Left.

Left: The South-west junction of the choir-stalls between S3 and S4
On a shield supported by two lions is a rampant lion crowned. Whittingham points out that these are the arms of Sir Thomas Morley who died in 1415, silver a lion rampant sable crowned, supported by lions.

Centre

A man and woman stand side by side. The woman on the left holds a book in both hands. She wears a cloak whose drawn-up folds reveal the drapery of her dress beneath. The heads of both man and woman have been sliced away. The man who is on the right has a cloak which falls in folds to below his knees, his stockinged legs showing beneath. He holds by both hands a scroll which falls to the right. Under the ledge of the misericord on the right a crown is carved with W, standing for William, the christian name of the man who stands beneath. A greyhound wearing a collar lies at the feet of the man and woman. In the Middle Ages the greyhound was considered as the aristocrat of dogs. Henry V1 used a greyhound as a support to his coat of arms. Here the coats of arms on the supporters identify the two figures as Sir William Clere of Ormesby, who died in 1384, and his wife Denise Wichingham.

Supporters

Left: A shield bearing the Clere coat of arms: silver on a fesse azure 3 eagles gold.

Right: A shield bearing the Wichingham arms: Ermine on a chief sable 3 crosses patée gold. In this Wichingham shield the ermine appears in the form of seven feathers. Both shields are hanging by straps.

It is not clear whether or not misericords were painted in the MiddleAges. It would seem that where so many shields appeared, as among the Norwich misericords, the probablility of their being painted, so that the colours could emphasize the necessary distinctions, would be high.

Elbow-rests

Right: As for S3 Left.

Left: A man holds a shield in front of him with a coat of arms. The shield is attached to him by shoulder straps. The arms are: sable a cross engrailed gold with a bendlet. Lions are carved either side of the shield-bearer. These are the arms of Sir Robert Ufford of Wrentham who died in 1392.

Centre

An impressive dragon with spread wings, and a whorled horn in the middle of its forehead. The dragon's beard falls either side of its face in tusk-like coils. The dragon's left wing, growing out of the left leg, seems unattached to the dragon's body. Its front, spine and tail are beaded. It stands on its victim whose head is missing. Oak leaves form the background.

Supporters

Both supporters are of a lion's head. They look like gargoyles. On the Left the lion's head has very large ears and its tongue hangs out. The Right is similar, but over its head it has two, not three twirls of hair, looking like horns.

Elbow Rests

Right: As for S4 Left.

Left: An angel emerging from the clouds of heaven holds a soul, in the form of a young child, in a napkin. The soul has its hands held together in prayer. A cross is carved above the angel's coronet. This sometimes denotes archangelic status, which in this case would indicate the Archangel Michael. This carving most probably represents the angel presenting to heaven the soul of Richard Courtenay, Bishop of Norwich 1413-15.

Centre

A cleric is seated. His hood covers the top and sides of his head. The fringe of his hair is seen beneath the cowl. He holds in his lap, by both hands, an open book whose pages face outwards. Above his head to the left is carved the letter R, and above his head to the right is carved the letter C. Each letter is surmounted by a crown. The cleric represented is Richard Courtenay, Bishop of Norwich 1413-15. He died of dysentery in attendance on King Henry V at Harfleur. He claimed kinship with the king. (8) This is perhaps a unique instance where a misericord carving of a bishop can be positively identified.

Supporters

Left: A shepherd is surrounded by ten sheep. He caresses one of the sheep with both hands. Two rams have their horns locked together. Beneath the shepherd's right foot is a feeding bowl.
Right: Two scholars sit with their books open. To the right two other scholars appear to be sporting. The heads of all four boys are missing. Above, a tonsured monk is preparing a meal. He is bending over a very large basket. A storage pot with a lid on is to his left. These supporters emphasize the pastoral duties undertaken by Bishop Courtenay who in fact did not visit his diocese. (8)

Elbow-rests

Right: As for S5 Left.

Left: An old man with flowing hair and beard. The crown, carved above his forehead and merging into the curve of the rest, marks him as a king.

Centre

Two woodwose men with hairy, leaf-like cladding, fight each other with cudgels held in their outside hands. With their inside hands they clutch at each other's faces. The one on the right pulls at the beard of his adversary, and the one on the left thrusts at the other's hair. Of their four legs three have broken off. Wild hairy men appear elsewhere in the cathedral's carving: in other misericords (S11, S28, N31), and in a roof boss in the north walk of the cloister. In the Middle Ages they were seen often in pageants as figures representing the wild men of the woods, satyrs, or fauns. The woodwose also became a popular supporter to some coats of arms. The dressing up as woodwoses was even undertaken at court: in 1460 by the King of France and his knights, and by the court of King Henry VIII. Froissart gives an account of five noblemen who dressed themselves in flax as wild men for a wedding feast at the court of Charles VI of France in 1393. When the Duke of Orleans approached with a torch to discover their identity, their costumes caught fire and resulted in the death of four of the 'wild men'. (6)

Supporters

Both supporters are of a stiff-leaf pattern set in the thin rib which curls down from the ledge.

Elbow-rests

Right: As for S6 Left.

Left: An old man's head whose hair and beard terminate in pointed leaves. Leaves are also growing out of his ears.

Centre

A mounted knight rides on a horse not large enough to carry the weight of the man. It would seem that the tail of a dragon is curled by the horse's rear legs, and part of its diminutive body appears to the right of the horse. The knight's right arm is raised as though wielding a lance. The representation is of St George and the dragon, but the proportions are unhappily executed. The knight stands erect in his stirrups, with his left hand on the reins. He wears no helmet, but he has an abundant head of hair and a neatly trimmed moustache and beard. The head of the horse has broken off. The carving behind the knight has the semblance of foliage.

Supporters

Left: These are the arms of Sir Thomas Hoo who took part in the battle of Agincourt, and who died in 1420. Whittingham notes that they depict those of an elder son before his father's death in 1410: quarterly silver and sable with label (a label of three points normally denotes an eldest son in the lifetime of his father). Sir Thomas's arms impale those of his first wife, Eleanor Felton, who died in 1400: red two lions passant ermine.

Right: Sir Thomas's mother was an heiress of the family of St Omer of Brundall, and her arms appear here: azure a fesse between 6 cross crosslets or. Both coats of arms hang by straps with buckles and eyelets.

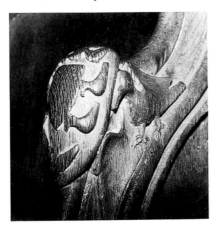

Elbow-rests

Right: As for S7 Left.

Left: The arms of Sir Thomas Erpingham who also fought at the battle of Agincourt. He died in 1428. Green a scutcheon in an orle of Martlets silver. A bird is carved either side of the rest.

Centre

A bear and a lion standing on their hind legs prepare to fight each other. The right foreleg of the bear is broken, and the left foreleg of the lion is damaged. The bear is wearing a collar. Both animals, with their fore-paws extended towards each other, are seen against a background of foliage.

Supporters

Left: A seated bear wearing a collar and chain.
Right: A seated squirrel also wearing a collar is eating a nut. The squirrel's tail follows the curve of its back and reaches to its head. For both supporters there is a background of foliage.

Elbow-rests

Right: As for S8 Left.

Left: A shield charged with red a saltire engrailed silver. These are the arms of Sir Leonard Kerdeston who died some time after 1421. Leaves curl backwards on to the elbow-rest.

Centre

A man and woman stand side by side. The figure on the left is the woman. She holds her hands together in prayer. A rosary is at her girdle. Her gown is buttoned to the neck. Her face has been sliced off but on her head are the remains of a wide-fronted head-dress. The man on the right has his right hand on his companion's shoulder as though comforting her. With his left hand he holds his girdle. A pair of gloves hang from his girdle and also a long dagger. Round his waist he wears a long belt the end of which is looped over at the waist and falls to beneath his knees. This part is studded with beads and terminates in a cross. The man's face, too, has been sliced off but the signs of a beard remain. He wears pointed shoes.

Supporters

The shields which serve as supporters identify the woman as Denise Wichingham, who died in 1390, the mother of the man who stands next to her, John Clere. The Clere family are frequently mentioned in the Paston Letters.

Left: A shield ermine with an indented chief sable charged with three crosses formy silver. (Wichingham)

Right: A shield silver a fesse azure with three eagles gold thereon. The arms of Clere of Ormseby. (7)

Elbow-rests

Right: As for S9 Left.

Left: The arms of Sir Robert Berney who died in 1415: per pale red and azure a cross engrailed ermine with a crescent. Foliage appears to the left of the arms. The Berneys also feature prominently in the Paston Letters.

Centre

A woodwose, a wild man, holds two chained lions on a leash. He has abundant curly hair and a beard that falls in symmetrical waves to just above his waist. He is clad in a ribbed garment that reaches to his ankles. A girdle passes round his waist. His feet are unshod. In his right hand he holds, parallel to the under-ledge of the misericord, a very large knobbly club. With his left hand he holds the leash which is attached to the two lions. The pulling of the chain seems to have turned this lion's head through an angle of 180 degrees. One of the lions is positioned under his right arm, and seems to be clawing at the woodwose's right knee. The other lion reaches up from the ground at the foot of the woodwose. This lion's head is missing. On the underside of the ledge is a scroll on which is written 'War Foli Wat', which might be translated as 'Beware of folly, man'. The allegorical meaning of the carving might be that it is imperative for man, even in a wild state, to control the animal forces that surge up in him and can destroy him.

Supporters

Left: A woodwose wrenching open the jaws of a lion.
Right: Two sheep, back to back, turning their heads inward.

Elbow-rests

Right: As for S10 Left.

Left: A shield: red a chevron between 3 fleur-de-lys gold. Leaves are carved either side of the shield.   These are the arms of Sir James Havile of Dunston who died in 1354.

Centre

The head of a king bearded and crowned. The strawberry leaves at the top of the crown curve outwards to accommodate the under-ledge of the misericord. The crown is decorated by a number of jewels in quatrefoil settings. The king's eyes are either closed or his look is downwards. Thick waves of hair come from under the crown, and his ample moustache and beard descend in patterned waves. The carving is of the highest quality. Whittingham ascribes the face to King Henry V (1948) and later to King Henry IV (1981. (23, 24)

Supporters

Left and Right is a stiff-leaf pattern.

Elbow-rests

Right: As for S11 Left

Left: A shield: azure a fesse between 3 leopards heads gold. Leaves are carved either side of the shield. These are the arms of Michael de la Pole, the 2nd Earl of Suffolk, who died of dysentery at Harfleur in 1415.

Centre

An eagle in winged flight lights upon an animal that has lost its head. It could be a doe or a lamb. The eagle has the talons of its left foot spread out upon the animal's back. The talons of its right foot are upon the back of a dove. The right leg of the eagle is missing. Its tail is also missing. The hooked beak of the eagle would have been pecking at the head of the animal. The allegorical meaning of the carving might imply the predatory power of the strong and ruthless crushing the young and innocent.

Supporters

On each side is a man's face looking towards the centre. The shaping of the neck indicates that these are profiles of a death mask. Both heads are set within the thin curved rib which comes from the inner edge of the ledge.

Left: On the head is a coif which falls over the back of the head and is kept in place by a linen ring. Ugly vertical segments of hair fall between ear and chin. The mouth is open, the teeth are showing, and the expression is one of a menacing snarl, altogether consonant with the action of the eagle in the centre of the misericord.

Right: The head, in its physiognomy, is similar to that on the Left. But the expression is one of repose. Such a head is to be seen on a misericord in St Katherine's-by-the-Tower. (19)

Elbow-rests

Right: As for S12 Left.

Left: The semblance of a bearded Green Man with shoots coming out of his mouth which form into very large leaves behind his head.

Centre

A wyvern has its head thrust upwards beneath the ledge of the seat. Its eye looks sidewards at the viewer. Its long tongue is pushed forwards out of its mouth, and its left ear curls upwards behind its head. Its wings are wide-spread, and its tail curls round on itself. The lower part of the wyvern's body is covered with defensive scales.

Supporters

Left and Right: Wyverns in upward flight. The designs are set within a circle.

Elbow-rests

Right: As for S13 Left.

Left: A man sitting on a stool holding the sides of his open jerkin, the bottom edges of which are dagged. He wears shoes with long turned-up points. His head is thrust back so that the round brim of his hat and the material that flows from the top of it are aligned to the rising curve of the elbow-rest.

Centre

An angel is seated on a bench-seat. He is crowned and wears a scapular with a hood attached.
His wings are spread wide on either side.   His right arm and hand are missing.   He would
have been holding in each hand a scroll, part of which has also disappeared.   This carving
represents the Angel of St Matthew.   This image of St Matthew, 'the winged living creature'
is derived from Revelation 4. 6-8.

Supporters

On either side is an angel with wings spread. Each angel faces the centre and is in movement as
though on an urgent mission. The angel on the Right has his left leg and foot missing.   The
carving is set within a circle.

Elbow-rests

Right: As for S14 Left.

Left: A man sitting on a stool holding a
leathern bottle.   His left shoe is long and
pointed.   His toes stick out of his right
shoe.

Centre

Two men are wrestling.   They wear short tunics, tied at the waist, and are bare-legged.   The wrestler on the left has his sleeves rolled up.   Both wear collars, a convention for this type of wrestling.   The man on the left grasps his opponent's collar with both hands; the man on the right has only one hand on the collar of the other.   On either side are seconds or, more likely, referees who stand by to see fair play.   Each lays one hand on the collar of the wrestler nearest to him, as though restraining him.   They seem dressed alike, but the one on the right has his head and one of his legs missing.   His opposite number has a leg missing but, from his bee-hive hat and girdled, pleated tunic with hanging sleeves, he figures as a gentleman of fashion.   Trees form the background.   In the first bay of the west walk of the cloister, nearest the former refectory, is a roof boss of two woodwose wrestling, each trying to grasp the chain around the other's neck.

Supporters

Left: A boar, with a ridged back, tusk, and pronounced genitals, wears a collar round its neck. Its right rear leg is missing. Two trees are in the background. The boar, set within a thin circular rib, appears to be setting off for the wrestling match.

Right: A swan with half-spread wings stands within a similar thin ribbed circle. The swan has a coronet round its throat.   It can be compared with the swan with the gorged crown in the vaulting of the first bay (counting from the east) of the nave. This emblem was one of the badges of the House of Lancaster at the time of the carving.

Elbow-rests

Right: As for S15 Left.

Left: A man at table holding his thighs. He wears a voluminous cloth hat, bound like a turban, but with large lappets. His tunic is short and exposes his thighs and legs.   The lower parts of his legs are cross-gartered. His shoes have pointed toes.

Centre

Two men fighting with a lion. The lion is in the centre and rampant, attacking the man on the right. The carving is well executed. The man on the left, who raises his club to bring it down on the head of the lion, also clutches the lion's mane with his left hand. Yet his position is relatively static when compared with the struggle of the lion with the man on the right. Each of these figures is balanced against the other in a complementary way. One of the lion's claws is thrust against the man's thigh, while the man's left foot pushes back the lion's loins. Both men wear close-fitting round hats, and knee-length tunics with hanging sleeves. The drawers are seen through the split skirt tunic of the man on the right. Both men are barefoot.

Supporters

Left and Right: On either side a ribbed-backed wyvern in a circular design.

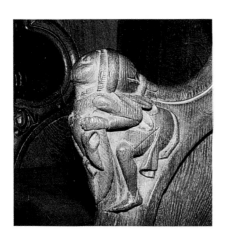

Elbow-rests

Right: As for S16 Left.

Left: A man, with a fancy hat with a bobble on top, is holding a shield in front of him on which are three pilgrims' shoes.(23) He wears a knee-length tunic and pointed shoes.

Centre

In the middle sits a man wearing a fool's hat and shoulder-cape. His arms, legs and feet are bare. He holds in both hands the rear legs of an animal. The middle part of the animal passes under his right arm. Its face has been sliced off leaving the outline which resembles that of a pig. The docked tail of the pig is turned upward as though presenting to the fool the chanter of a bagpipe, while the bag of the instrument, the pig's body, is squeezed underneath the fool's right arm. A dog to the left looks on grinning. On the right, seated in the branches of a tree, is a bear with a chain round its neck. It is holding a scourge in the form of a bunch of birch twigs in its right paw. Foliage is carved behind the dog and the bear. At the base of the composition are two holes, one either side of the fool's feet. In the hole on the left are seen the rear-quarters of an animal, it might be that of a dog, and peeping out from the hole on the right is the head perhaps of the same dog. No dachshund even could possibly be that long. A contemporary misericord, in the church of St Peter and St Paul, Lavenham, Suffolk, has such a scene of merrymaking in which a jester holds a pig as though playing the bagpipes on the animal. (12)

Supporters:

Left: A seated bear with a chain round its neck attached to an hour-glass. The bear plays a pipe which it holds to its mouth with both hands. **Right:** Another seated bear much defaced.

Elbow-rests

Right: As for S17 Left.

Left: A man, wearing a hat, tunic and pointed shoes, bears a shield charged with a cross of sprouting twigs which Whittingham describes as 'pilgrim's crossed staves'. The shield-bearer wears a large hat, short tunic and pointed shoes.

S19 No misericord

Elbow-rests

Right: As for S18 Left.

Left: A seated figure with chin held up and head thrust back, holding in front of him with both hands a shield with no discernible markings. His tunic is scalloped with billowing sleeves. The tunic is cut away by the thighs showing a length of leg and a pointed ankle boot. On the west side the carving has been removed to accommodate a door fitment.

Centre

The face of a Green Man is carved with hawthorn branches coming from above his eyes and from above his mouth. These branches break into luxuriant leaf, creating an impressive symmetrical pattern on either side, and narrowing at the base to a pointed foliate beard. Three tendrils with triangular ends are affixed to the Green Man's forehead. His face is that of a young man: smooth, full-lipped, wide-eyed. The Green Man is frequently associated with hawthorn leaves. The hawthorn, or may, which reputedly blossoms on the 1st May, is a concomitant of the old year renewing itself in Spring, and the May ceremonies, such as dancing round the Maypole, May Games, and the rites of Spring, are sometimes celebrated by the covering of the head in wreaths of flowers or foliage. Many of the cloister bosses depict Green Men, but there is no stone carving of Green Men within the Cathedral, although they are to be seen, for instance, among the bosses in the nave of Winchester Cathedral, and in the vaulting of the Lady Chapel in Ely Cathedral. It might be that by the time the nave vaulting was erected at Norwich, beginning c1465, images of the pagan Green Men were confined to wooden carvings beneath the choir-stall seats.

Supporters

Left and Right: Hawthorn leaves set in a diamond pattern.

Elbow-rests

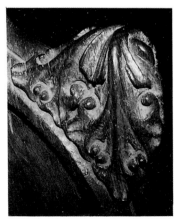

Right: Carving of foliage.
Left: A man wears a head-dress which covers his ears, and which has pleated folds of cloth at the back. He wears a short tunic, and he holds in front of him a round hat with a brim. He is seated upon a stool. His short ankle-boots have pointed toes.

27

Centre

This carving of an owl mobbed by five starlings is reputedly one of the finest of English misericords. The owl is perched amidst the branches of a vine. At the level of the owl's head are seen on either side vine leaves and bunches of grapes. A criss-cross pattern is carved between the top of the vine and the underside of the seat's ledge. The owl has its eyes open and stares straight ahead. It is being pecked by five birds, two either side and one beneath. The design preserves a pleasing symmetry. In the Middle Ages the owl frequently represents the Synagogue, the Jewish Church, which when offered the light of Christ's teaching preferred darkness. In the north walk of the cloister there are two bosses in the vaulting, both showing an owl perched in a pear tree.

Supporters

Both supporters, set within a roundel, show an eagle with wings extended pecking at the head of another bird, which Whittingham identifies as a dove.

Elbow-rests

Right: As for S20 Left.

Left: A man with his hat swept back. He has flowing wing-like sleeves. He holds a shield in front of him with his right hand. Behind him in his left hand he holds a knobbly club. His legs pass through the holes of a ledge as though he is standing in the stocks. The shield rests on the ledge.

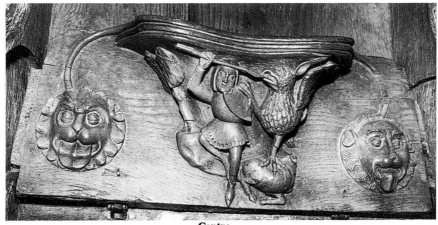

Centre

A fight is taking place between a man and a griffin.   The griffin, a mythical creature which is usually depicted with the head, wings and fore-talons of an eagle and the rear parts of a lion, has here extremely long and pointed ears.   The griffin has the talons of its left foot spread upon the body of a lamb which it has apparently subdued.   The lion's part of the griffin, its rear quarters, legs and tail are carved beneath the extended left wing. The talons of the griffin's right leg are thrusting back the warrior's shield, which is triangular in shape and notched on the top edge as though to receive a couched lance.   The man is thrusting the tip of his spear into the griffin's mouth. Some of the details of his dress are exquisitely carved: the buttons on the right arm, and the edging decoration at the bottom of his jerkin, creating an impression of a leather garment.   The tunic is drawn in at the waist.   The man wears a cowled hat and short boots. In medieval iconography there are many examples of men fighting griffins, one such occurs as a stone carving in the vaulting of the west walk of the cloister at Norwich. The representation is that of the griffin, as a force of evil, seeking to overcome man, who fights for the forces of good. The threatened lamb in this misericord stresses the man's task as righteous rescuer. A magnificent griffin is also to be seen as a roof boss carved in the nave, second bay from the east.

Supporters

Left: A lion's head carved in a roundel. The lion grimaces fiercely with its tongue thrust out of its mouth.

Right: A lion's head similar to that above.

Elbow-rests

Right: As for S21 Left.

Left: A man whose head-dress lies in long folds over his head. He wears a short tunic, showing his thighs and legs. His shoes have long pointed toes. His jerkin is pleated. He holds between his knees a shield on which a head is carved. In his right hand he holds a rod or scroll.

Centre

The Lion of St Mark stands with its wings wide-spread.   Its legs are braced upon a curved branch. Its tail sweeps round between its hind legs and over its back. From the lion's mouth comes the beginning of a scroll, St Mark's Gospel.

Supporters

Each is a patterned square of foliage set within a circle.

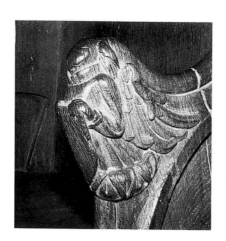

Elbow-rests

Right: As for S22 Left.

Left: An angel, emerging from the clouds, is wearing an amice and holds a shield in front of him.

Centre

The ox of St Luke with a scroll in its mouth. The ox is horned and winged with a furled tail that rises vertically. The ox is in a lying position. The scroll winds from the ox's mouth and extends even below the ox to the extent of its body. The scroll represents St Luke's Gospel.

Supporters

Each supporter is of an angel's head wearing a coronet with a frontal ornament.

Elbow-rests

Right: As for S23 Left.

Left: A man seated in a short tunic, drawn in at the waist. His hands are behind his bottom. In front of him is a shield on which is the representation of a bearded man with his tongue hanging out.

Centre

In the centre of the carving is a monk in a skull cap. He is seated and wears a scapular and long gown. He is apparently acting as a schoolmaster and small boys are gathered around him. One boy is held over his knees. The boy's bottom is bare, and the master has his hand on the boy's bare back. The master's right hand and arm are missing. Part of a strap is to be seen over his right shoulder. Two trees are set on either side. Also either side are two schoolboys with their books open. All five heads of the boys are missing. The master's head has also been damaged.

Supporters

For each supporter is carved a boy or man in a long gown with a girdle. In each case the head is missing. The carving is set within a whirling scroll. The birching of a schoolboy is the subject of a misericord in Sherborne Abbey. The supporters are schoolboys, with faces like monkeys, busy with their books.

Elbow-rests

Right: As for S24 Left.

Left: The head of an old bearded man. The drapery from his hat hangs down in long folds.

Centre

The carving is of a powerful bull which twists its head backwards on its shoulders. Its mouth is open and it shows its teeth menacingly. Its horns curl backwards. Its left ear is very large and twirls upwards. Matted hair lies like a carpet over its shoulders. Its long tail is twisted through its hind legs and its knobbled end, like a distaff, lies on the animal's rump. The legs of the bull, contrary to the whole appearance of the beast, are doubled up underneath it, in a position of repose. It is probable that the bull here is representing Taurus, one of the signs of the Zodiac.

Supporters

Both Left and Right are of a stylized leaf.

Elbow-rests

Right: As for S25 Left.

Left: An eagle with its head and neck bent backwards is preening its back feathers.

Carved on the edge of the seat, spaced at intervals, are four diamonds set in squares. This according to Whittingham is one of the signs of the work being undertaken after the fire of 1509. Tracy agrees with this view but points out that the style and workmanship is in keeping with that at the beginning of the 15th century.

Centre

A woman is in the centre. The drapes of her head-dress cover her ears and fall to her shoulders. She wears an apron and a sleeveless gown. An empty pot hangs to the left of her head, and beneath the pot is a ladle. To the right of the pot are two birds, each with one wing spread. Behind the woman a large store pot into which a pig, with an unusually large and splayed tail, has buried his snout. The woman, holding her distaff in her broken hand, has turned to chase a fox who runs away with a goose whose head is lodged in the fox's mouth. Below, a dog chases the fox. Between the fox's tail and the dog is a dead bird. Above the dead bird is a spindle which the woman has just let fall from her right hand. The branches and foliage of trees form the background to what appears to be a farm-yard scene. Whittingham entitles this misericord Sloth, one of the Seven Deadly Sins. He also likens the scene to that depicted by Chaucer in the Nun's Priest's Tale. Certainly, the intense activity in the farm-yard, including 'Malkyn, with a dystaf in hir hand' somewhat resembles Chaucer's description of the great chase that followed the fox's seizure of Chauntecleer. But the ascription to Sloth is doubtful. The carver has chosen to portray one of the many escapades of the popular medieval romance of Reynard the Fox.

Supporters

Left and Right: Rose patterns.

Elbow-rests

Right: As for S26 Left.

Left: A winged angel with long curly hair has his hands resting on his waist.

Centre

On the left is a wild man and on the right is a lion. The man is almost naked apart from the covering of his loins. He has long hair over which is a plaited wreath. He holds a club in his right hand. The club is spiralled, wide at the mid point and tapering to the end. Tree foliage forms the background to the club. The wild man's left forearm and hand are missing. It would appear that he is leading the lion which he has tamed. The lion has a collar around its neck but the chain that was attached to it has been broken off. The lion is broad-breasted with a full mane. Its slim rear-quarters slope up towards the underside of the seat ledge. The ridge of the lion's back is beaded.

Supporters

On each side is a lion, curled and couchant, with crossed hind legs.

Elbow-rests

Right: As for S27 Left.

Left: A jester's face with a scalloped edging to his head-dress, which has rose patterns over the ears. The collar has a double row of scallops.

Centre

A lion with full mane is snarling. It is lying down. Its tail twists round the middle of its body and rises vertically above the level of the lion's head. The tail ends in a broad spiral. Perhaps the lion represents Leo, another sign of the Zodiac.

Supporters

On each side is a carving of a stiff-leaf pattern.

Elbow-rests

Right: As for S28 Left.

Left: A pot-bellied, long-haired man with a curly beard. His hands are carefully carved on either side at waist level.

The edge of the seat is carved with the diamond patterns that indicate that at least some of the work is post 1509.

Centre

A bearded man dressed in a Robin Hood styled hat rides on the back of an antlered deer. With his right hand he holds the left antler, and in his left hand he carries an animal like a squirrel. He wears a netted tunic, and boots that reach to below his knees, but his toes are exposed Behind him are two snarling hounds. In front of the deer is an animal with the head of a sheep and the brush of a fox. Whittingham (1981) describes this carving as 'Lechery in net on hart'.(24) The carving might depict Lechery by showing the beastliness of man in his close association with the animals. Here the rider clutches the horns of the deer. The horns themselves are a symbol of adultery. Falstaff, who finds himself playing the part of Herne the Hunter in *The Merry Wives of Windsor*, with a deer's mask on his head, is punished in this form for his lechery.

Supporters

Left and Right: A blemya, a monstrous human form in which the head appears below the level of the shoulders. Othello, in telling Desdemona of his travels, speaks of 'The Anthropophagi, and men whose heads/ Do grow beneath their shoulders' (I.iii.144). And the Host in *The Merry Wives of Windsor* says that Falstaff, the beastly knight, will speak like an Anthropophaginian (IV.v. 10). Each figure wears a short-skirted tunic with puffed shoulders and carries a dagger in the right hand. And each has long pointed shoes. Such figures appear and are named Blemyes in the African section of the late thirteenth century Mappa Mundi. They appear also in other misericord supporters, such as that in the Victoria and Albert Museum. (12)

Elbow-rests

Right: A long-haired, bearded warrior is in the jaws of a monster. Only the upper part of the man is visible. He is clad in armour which covers his shoulders and elbows, and a breast-plate protects his chest. The monster has four beads set vertically on its forehead. Its eyes are open and its long ears are curved backwards.

Left: A man wearing a garment open at the neck and with long puffed sleeves which, held by a ring above the elbow, fan out behind. On the right the cloak is knotted. In front of the man a pestle is set in a jug with ringed handles.

Centre

A wyvern with its head raised towards the underside of the ledge of the misericord. Its tongue is sticking out, and its large, left, pointed ear extends to just above its tail which curls back on itself and is broken at the end. Its two feet are webbed. The body of the wyvern is pitted. The carving gives the impression of power and movement. The wyvern is distinguished from the dragon by having two legs instead of four. Its tail is often represented as being barbed.

Supporters

Right: The face of a bald-headed man with large ears. He has a moustache which extends from the corners of his nose to the sides of his face. There is a trace of a beard. He is grinning and showing his teeth.
Left: Another face of a bald-headed man, but there are bunches of hair above his ears. He has a spiralling moustache, with also a trace of a beard.

Elbow-rests

Right: As for S30 Left.

Left: A figure, bearded and bald, in the jaws of a monster. From his hat, which is set at the back of his head, flows a piece of cloth. The shoulders of his tunic are puffed and slashed.

Centre

An antelope has its head thrust up against the underside of the ledge of the misericord. Its mouth is open as it looks upwards. On its left shoulder, the one exposed to the viewer, is a circular protrusion that would serve the animal as a protective shield when it charges its foe. The two horns of the antelope are long and straight with spiralled markings. The beast has a broad and wavy tail. There is a hint of foliage above and in front of the antelope. According to the medieval bestiaries the antelope has two powerful horns in order to saw through trees. The horns represent the Old and the New Testaments against which the devil is powerless. Some antelopes are shown with serrated horns which clearly enhance their sawing ability. In this Norwich misericord the spiralled horns might act more like drills than saws. The antelope is to be seen on the vaulting above the tomb of Henry V in Westminster Abbey. The heraldic antelope, the yale, is also used in the arms of Henry IV's third son, John, Duke of Bedford, who is buried in Rouen Cathedral, and later in the 15th century it is seen upholding the Beaufort badge of a crowned portcullis.

Supporters
Left and Right: A large roundel containing a curling leaf.

Elbow-rests

Right: As for S31 Left.

Left: A page kneels with a shield in front of him. His instep follows the curve of the rest so that the soles of his shoes are showing. His short tunic has a collar and a flared skirt. The details of his face and the markings on his shield have been smoothed away with age. His hair is set in a roll at the back of his head.

Centre

The main figure is of a portly man with a long staff which he wields in front of him. He wears no hat. His head is bald on top, but ample hair grows from the back of his head. He is bearded and moustached. His cloak passes over his left shoulder, and a pouch hangs from his belt on that side. He wears a full-skirted tunic and ankle boots into which his leggings are tucked. Behind him is a dog who puts his fore-paw on the man's cloak. In front are two more dogs, both menacing. A tree stands between the man and the front two dogs. It is as though the man is trying to defend himself from the threatening dogs by brandishing his staff. All the dogs have their tails curling upwards. The man's left hand has been broken off. Whittingham's description of this misericord (1981) is 'Vanity overclad beats bushes in vain'. (24) The main figure is certainly in appearance like the stage appearance of Falstaff, 'that vanity of years'.

Supporters

Left and Right: A circular leaf pattern.

Elbow-rests

Right: As for S32 Left.

Left: An eagle with two heads bends its two necks backwards to bite each side of the rest. It is a fine and unusual carving.

Misericords of the north side of the choir, transept and sanctuary.

N1 A misericord representing Norwich Football Club with Bryan Gunn saving a goal. Not illustrated. (Installed in 2001)

Elbow-rests

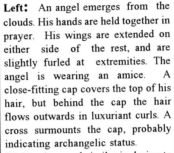

Left: An angel emerges from the clouds. His hands are held together in prayer. His wings are extended on either side of the rest, and are slightly furled at extremities. The angel is wearing an amice. A close-fitting cap covers the top of his hair, but behind the cap the hair flows outwards in luxuriant curls. A cross surmounts the cap, probably indicating archangelic status.
Right: An angel similar in design to that on the Left, with amice, cap surmounted by cross, and flowing hair at the back. But this angel holds a shield in front of him, charged with a cross, the arms of the Priory: silver a cross sable (see Right elbow-rest N17). The stall N1, the first return stall on the north side, is not attached to the next stall, N2.

N2 A misericord representing the University of East Anglia. Not illustrated. (Installed in 2001)

Elbow-rests

Left: The face of an old man with wavy hair and beard. A fillet binds his brows. A repair has been carried out on top of the rest. On the right side of this rest is a hawk with extended wing. The hawk's curved beak pecks at the back of the man's head.
Right: An angel holding a rebec in front of him with both hands. The bare toes of the angel are seen on either side. The angel's wings are spread, and they sweep backwards towards the rest in line with the angel's head

Centre

The front edge of the misericord has been damaged. Below are two angels in flight, their wings spreading out from the clouds beneath the misericord ledge. They have curled hair and look outward. With both hands they grasp a large crown that would fit more than comfortably on to the head of the Virgin Mary who sits below. She has long wavy hair, parted in the middle, which flows either side of her shoulders.   She wears an overmantle with capacious sleeves which is fastened at chest level. The carving of the folds of her gown at knee-level is done with great care. With her two hands she holds the Christ-child who sits naked on her lap. Her left hand holds his thigh and her right the toes of his right foot. The child's head is missing. The child holds an object in his hands which Whittingham takes to be a dove.

The scene depicts the Coronation of the Virgin in which the angels rather than Christ are placing the crown on her head. It is one of the few representations of religious subjects among the Norwich Cathedral misericords. It might be because this was at one time the Chancellor's or an archdeacon's stall.

Supporters

Another reason why the subject of the central carving relates to the Christian faith might be because the donor, Isabella Beauchamp, a daughter of the Earl of Warwick (d. 1397), was a nun. But before becoming a nun she had been married twice, first to John Lestrange who died in 1375, and secondly to William de Ufford, Earl of Suffolk, who died in 1382. Isabella died in 1416. The arms of her two husbands, hanging by straps with buckles and eyelets, are carved on the supporters.

Left: The arms of the Earl of Suffolk are here represented as sable a cross engrailed gold with a bendlet sinister for difference.(7)

Right: The arms of John Lestrange are: red 2 lions silver, the field powdered with stars for difference.(23)

Elbow-rests

Left: As for N2 Right.
Right: The angle carving N3/N4 between the return stalls and the south-facing stalls on the north side. (See opposite page.)

The North-west junction of the choir stalls between N3 and N4

At the angle between N3, which is the last return stall on the north side facing east, and N4, the first stall at the west end on the north side facing south, is a carving of a king's head. Whittingham (1981) identifies this as representing King Henry IV (1399-1413).(24) If the carving of the Wakering stalls was carried out in 1420, when Henry V was reigning, the portrayal of his father's head in this position would be a reasonable possibility.

The carving itself is a remarkable piece of work. It does not comprise part of a misericord, but is permanently visible in its corner position between N3 and N4. In dimensions it is larger than the misericord carvings. It shows a noble head wearing a crown with strawberry leaf decorations. The king's hair from beneath the crown on either side sweeps in serpentine waves from the side of the forehead down to the level of the moustache which is long, wavy, and interestingly asymmetrical, being longer on the right side. The magnificent beard divided in the front, echoes the undulations of the moustache. The waves of the hair which are swept to the side of the head terminate in little knots. The eyes look downwards. The end of the nose has been sliced off. The broad forehead and the high cheek bones enhance the majestic mien. Above all the grain marks of the oak on the forehead and beneath the eyes leave a deep impression of power and nobility. It is doubtful whether this carving of a king's head is intended as a portrait. Certainly, it bears little resemblance to the alabaster effigy of Henry IV in Canterbury Cathedral (c. 1410-20).

Centre

A knight stands facing the front, but his feet are pointing to the left. His full head of hair reaches to the underside of the ledge of the misericord. His helmet is by his right shoulder. His right arm has been broken off. His moustache and beard are fashionably trimmed. His beard is forked. His armour is jointed and flexible. His waist is small and a girdle adorned with medallions is at hip level. He wears knee-armour, and foot armour, in flexible segments. With his left hand he holds the hilt of a sword encased in a scabbard which hangs down on the left side. The lower part of sword and scabbard have broken off. A band over his shoulders is attached to his shield which he carries on his left arm. The indentation at the top of the shield might indicate that it was used in jousts. A lance would be couched in such a notch. Behind him is slung a quiver with a sheaf of arrows, the tips of which are seen on the left of his hip. His shield is charged ermine with 2 chevronels sable. The knight has been identified as Sir Rober de Illey of Plumstead who died in 1392. It would appear that the donor of this seat was Elizabeth Felton, a neighbour of Sir Robert's. The arms of her two husbands appear in the supporters.

Supporters

Left: These are the arms of Elizabeth Felton' second husband, Sir Thomas Hoo of Brundall, who died in 1420. His arms impale those of Felton.

Right: The arms of Sir Robert de Ufford of Wrentham impaling those of Felton (see S8) sable a cross engrailed gold, a bendlet impaling red 2 lions passant ermine. Sir Robert died in 1392. Both coats of arms are hanging by straps; the Left one is marked with a buckle.

Elbow-rests

Left: The king's head appears here at the angle of the return stalls.

Right: A lion's face with the tongue sticking out. The lion's mane streams out behind.

Centre

A hunting scene of which the supporters form part. The hunter with curly hair, moustache, and beard, holds a curved hunting horn to his lips. Two bands, one above the man's hand and one below, are round the horn. The hunter is fashionably dressed in a short tunic with a row of buttons down the front, a girdle at hip-level, and a belt over his shoulders attached to his cloak. He wears long pointed shoes. He carries a quiver of arrows behind him. His left arm is missing. Under his right arm an open-mouthed stag is at bay, threatened by two hounds, both wearing collars. Another stag is behind him on his left.

Supporters

Left: A stag in flight. Its head is missing but it turns its neck as though to look at its pursuers.
Right: Two stags in flight. Both supporting carvings are informed with the sense of the speed of the chase.

Elbow-rests

Left: As for N4 Right.

Right: A man's face with streaming hair and beard.

Centre

The central figure is that of a standing naked man. His legs are broken off beneath the thighs. One foot remains which is placed upon a dragon. This dragon's wide-open mouth is biting the man's groin. The man's right hand is on the dragon's head. On the right a large lion with a full mane is biting the upper part of the man's left arm, while the man himself grasps the lion's paw. A wyvern with a curled tail bites the upper part of the man's right arm. The man has curly hair and a trimmed moustache. He is by no means a woodwose combating with the wild beasts. His appearance resembles that of St George in S8. Although he is assailed on every side there is no tension in the struggle nor evidence of pain. Instead, a slight smile plays about his mouth. In this context the dragon and the lion represent the forces of evil assailing, it would seem, the innocent.

Supporters

Left: Three finely-cut vine leaves.
Right: Two damaged vine leaves, the third has disappeared. Top right, a large bunch of grapes.

Elbow-rests

Left: As for N5 Right.

Right: A striking carving of an angel wearing a feathered costume. Most of his features have worn away. The angel rests on some clouds. His long wavy hair streams horizontally behind him, while his delicately-cut wings fall vertically along the curve of the rest.

Centre

A knight and his lady stand hand-in-hand. He is dressed in full armour from head to foot: he has helmet, gorget, hauberk, gauntlets, a medallioned belt at hip level from which his dagger hangs, articulated leg armour with knee pieces. At his foot is the head and front paw of a lion. He looks to the front. His lady looks modestly downward. She wears a coronet over her hair which is bunched at the sides and plaited in front. Her dress has a low, square-cut neck-line, close fitting to the waist, pleated below and with a train that can be seen between the knight's legs. The base of the skirt is swept gracefully to one side to reveal the head and front paws of a dog. The lady holds one hand to her breast and the other she has placed into her husband's gauntleted right hand. The work has been executed with great tenderness and skill. The supporters indicate that the couple are Sir William Wingfield of Letheringham in Suffolk, who died in 1378, and his wife, Margaret Boville.(7)

Supporters

Left: The Wingfield arms: Silver on a bend red 3 pairs of wings.
Right: The Boville arms: Quarterly gold and sable.
Both shields hang by straps.

Elbow-rests

Left: As for N6 Right.

Right: An angel with an eagle either side with heads turned to bury their beaks into the angel's wings. The eagles' talons are braced against the curved sides of the stall. The angel wears a feathered tunicle over a pleated alb. His hands are held together in prayer. His features have been worn smooth with age.

Centre

The figure of an angel emerges above a formal but asymmetric cloud. Clouds also are carved beneath the ledge of the misericord. The angel's head is missing. The wings of the angel sweep up to and are gracefully drawn down from, the under-ledge. They form a beautiful background to an exquisite composition for which the loss of the angel's head is deeply regretted. The part of the angel that is visible is clad in a feathered garment. The angel holds before him in both hands a large crown with a cross in front. The positioning of the hands is consonant with the elegance of the carving. The left hand supports the base of the crown and the right hand balances the upper part.

Supporters

Left and Right: Both supporters, each comprising an angel playing a musical instrument, are part of the overall composition. It is the sort of grouping of angels that is portrayed in medieval iconography as the preliminary to the Coronation of the Virgin. Unfortunately each of the angels is missing his head. Each angel, as the one in the centre, emerges from clouds. The angel on the Left plays on a psaltery. This is a stringed instrument played on the lap with two hands, the melody, apparently being plucked with the right hand and accompanied with the left. The markings on the psaltery are similar to that being played by King David, illustrated in the Psalter of Alfonso the Magnanimous, made in Italy c.1442, and now in the British Library. The angel on the Right plays on a rebec. The bow has been broken. (14) A misericord in Worcester Cathedral, late 14th century, showing men harvesting wheat, has as its supporters an angel on the Left playing the rebec, and an angel on the Right playing a psaltery.

Elbow-rests

Left: As for N7 Right.

Right: An eagle with spread wings has its face in profile looking east.

Centre

A mermaid with long wavy hair offers her right breast to a lion. She has a scaly tail which begins at her waist and curves up to the right beneath the lion. To the left, on the level of the mermaid's head, is a round mirror which hangs by a strap from a whorled conch the end of which has broken off. Beneath the mermaid are two small fish swimming in the sea. The head of the beast suckled is more like that of a cow than a lion, but the prominent mane, characteristic feet, and the context of the carving pronounce it to be lion. Other misericords in which a mermaid is suckling a lion are to be seen in Wells Cathedral and in Edlesborough, Buckinghamshire. The mermaid, often seen with mirror and comb, symbolizes a seductive force which tempts man to perdition. She assumes the power of the sirens who through music - and here the conch is significant - lead sailors to shipwreck. Like her classical counterpart, Venus, she is sometimes seen in the company of dolphins.(21) Oberon, too, recalls this association when he tells Puck that he 'heard a mermaid on a dolphin's back/ Uttering such dulcet and harmonious breath/ That the rude sea grew civil with her song'.*(A Midsummer Night's Dream.* II . i. 150*)*. In this carving the lion is not a symbol of nobility but of bestiality.

Supporters

Left and Right: A fierce faced dolphin, carved within a circle. Each has its mouth stretched open, and with its tail it is sweeping into its mouth a smaller dolphin. The power and savagery expressed by the carving of the supporters is an effective comment on the destiny of those that fall to the mermaid's blandishments. Fierce dolphins also act as supporters to the mermaid on a misericord in St Laurence's, Ludlow.

Elbow-rests

Left: As for N8 Right.

Right: The head of a man with snaky locks. His features have worn away.

Centre

An eagle with wings spread looks to the right and touches its wing with its curved beak. Its hooked talons firmly grasp the knobbly tree-trunk on which it perches. Its tail sweeps upwards gracefully. This is an elegant and balanced composition, splendidly positioned in the space available.

Supporters

Left: An old man's face, moustached and bearded. His wavy, serpentine hair frames his face. Heavy lobes are set on his forehead.

Right: A similar face to that on the Left, but this head is crowned.

Elbow-rests

Left: As for N9 Right.

Right: A lion's head and body appear either side of the rest. The lion has three legs on each side. It has two tails, one on either side of the elbow-rest, which pass under its belly and come together, as the ends proliferate, on top of the rest. The Left side is damaged.

Centre

St Michael overcomes the devil in the form of a dragon. 'And there was war in heaven: Michael and his angels fought against the dragon; and the dragon fought and his angels.' (Rev. 12.7) The carving of the Wakering choir-stalls took place at the same time that the bosses depicting the Apocalypse were being completed in the cloister. Here St Michael is seen with bare feet standing on the dragon. His left foot is firmly planted on the dragon's body. The seven small heads of the the dragon, at the end of their thin necks, are spread across the bottom of St Michael's shield. St Michael has three pairs of wings: one pair that is pointed and springs from his back to the under ledge of the misericord; one pair that is feathered, spreading out from behind him and curving downwards; and the the third pair which covers him as a skirt of which one wing is feathered and the other plumed. St Michael wields his sword in his right hand which is behind his head. The end of the sword has broken off. He wears shoulder straps, knotted in front. His shield which he thrusts downwards on to the dragon has a face carved on the front of it: two eyes, a snub nose, and a grinning mouth. There is a notch in the top of the shield in which a lance might be couched, indicating that it is for use in the lists.

Supporters

Left and Right: Formal leaf pattern attached to serpentine stem.

Elbow-rests

Left: As for N10 Right.

Right: A grimacing gnome or jester with a scalloped hood kneeling bent double, hands on knees.

Centre

A pelican with wings grandly spread feeds with its own blood its young which reach up towards it from their nest. This traditional composition of the pelican and its young is called 'the pelican in its piety'. The story about the pelican in Physiologus (22) is that the parent out of exasperation with its fledgelings kills them, but later has pity on them and brings them back to life by pecking its own breastand reviving them with it blood. The Christian parallel was with the Saviour, scourged and buffeted and, when placed on the cross and his side pierced by a spear, his blood flowed freely to redeem the children of men. 'The pelican in its piety' becomes the symbol of Christ's self-sacrificing love.(16) This symbol appears frequently in Norwich Cathedral: as a roof boss in the north walk of the cloister; as a carving for the hand-rest on the Bishop's stall, now the Dean's stall in the choir; as carvings in stone above alternate piers in the transepts; and on the late 14th century lectern under the crossing. The medieval craftsmen continued to depict the pelican in the form it appeared in the bestiaries probably long after the true shape of the pelican was generally known.

Supporters

Left and Right: A headless pelican on each side. Each with its wings half spread. On the Left a leg is broken although the claws remain.

Elbow-rests

Left: As for N11 Right.

Right: A gnome-like face with leaf ends. His arms curve backwards, and with his hands he is grasping his buttocks.

N13

Centre

Samson wrenches open the jaws of a lion. He stands against a background of foliage, struggling with the lion. He is dressed as a medieval knight. He wears no helmet but shows a full head of hair and also moustache and forked beard. His leather tunic is fastened down the front by thongs passing through the eyelets. Beneath the almost sleeveless tunic Samson is seen to be wearing chain-mail. His medallioned belt is at hip level. A chain encircles the top of his thigh. His knees are protected by armour. With his right hand he levers up by the nose the upper jaw of the lion while with his left hand, which is placed right inside the lion's mouth, he thrusts downwards. In his tussle with the lion he stands athwart the animal and looks outward. The carving of the lion reveals its extensive mane and a long tail that curves upwards and then behind Samson. It is probable that this misericord was being carved at the same time as the roof boss in the west walk of the cloister, on the same theme but in a very different style. The encounter in the cloister is much more threatening to Samson who has neither the handsome knightly apparel nor the cool assurance of victory seen in this misericord. Samson's struggle with the lion is in medieval iconography a prefiguring of Christ's overcoming evil.

Supporters

Left: A crane (?) whose head is missing, with very large talons contained within a circling stem. Its left leg is broken.

Right: A splendidly carved owl with a mouse in its beak. The owl too is contained within a circling stem. The left leg of the owl has broken off. The owl holds the mid part of the mouse in its beak: the mouse's buttocks and long tail are to the left and its long neck and head to the right. In the north walk of the cloister there are two roof boss carvings of an owl in a pear tree holding a mouse in its beak.

Elbow-rests

Left: As for N12 Right.

Right: A worn polished face from which triangular leaves grow on each side. From below the chin a stem turns back on itself in a complicated knot design.

Centre

A tree trunk and foliage form the background to an ape riding on the back of a dog. The dog has its head twisted round and upwards. Its mouth is open and it shows its teeth. The ape sits facing the back of the dog and holds a scourge, a bundle of rods, in its right hand. The ape's left hand has broken off, but with its hand it would have been holding the dog's tail, the end of which is over the ape's left arm. Monkeys appear very frequently on misericord carvings. They are known for their mimicry of man. They were trained to ride on horses and other sorts of animals as a village green entertainment.(5) Some modern commercial television advertisements are still exploiting the entertainment value of the monkey's mimicry of man! The monkey also features in the marginalia of some illuminated manuscripts, and in one such example a monkey is seated backwards riding on a goat. (*Peterborough Psalter*, Brussels)

Supporters

Left and Right: An ape carved within the curve of a circular stem looks on at the entertainment. Each is missing an arm and leg. Each ape has its mouth open and holds the side of its face. This is often a sign of toothache.

Elbow-rests

Left: As for N13 Right.

Right: A monkish face with cowl. He is attached, like a centaur, to the body of a four-legged animal, hooved like a horse. A tail on the left side curls under the body.

Centre

In the middle beneath the ledge of the misericord is carved a stylized a tree, and beneath the tree is an ox with its head tilted upwards. Its mouth is open. It appears to be resting under the tree. Three of its feet are visible, but they are clawed not hoofed. A quadrant of curled hair adorns its left shoulder like an epaulette. The ox's tail twists upwards away to the right.

Supporters

Left and Right: The supporters have been removed.

Elbow-rests

Left: As for N14 Right.

Right: A bald head with large ears and a sphinx-like face, with tongue hanging out. The body is that of an animal with four legs and cloven feet, a centaur.

N16

Centre

A man sits astride a wild boar in the act of drawing his sword. He represents Ira or Wrath, one of the Seven Deadly Sins. He wears a bee-hive hat, which has a ring at the top of it and an ornamented band above the brim. He holds his head on one side and grimaces, showing his teeth. His hair flows down to shoulder level. He is fashionably dressed with puffed shoulders to his tunic, over which is a narrowing plate of breast armour. The tunic has a short pleated skirt which reaches just below the thighs. Wrath wears elegant boots, heeled, split at the ankle, and with pointed toes. He is in the process of drawing his sword from a looped strap. The boar that carries him has its head tipped upwards, its mouth wide open, and it shows its tusks. Its back is ridged, its tail short and curled, and it appears to be moving at some speed. The wild boar is itself a symbol of wrath. Wrath as a Deadly Sin, is usually depicted as extremely aggressive and ready to strike in an indiscriminate way. (17)

Supporters

Left and Right: On each side a formalized circular leaf pattern with berries.

Elbow-rests

Left: As for N15 Right.

Right: An old man with a fringed beard and swept back hair. He wears a long gown with a collar, capacious sleeves that fall behind him, with puffed and slashed shoulders. He holds in both hands a bag slightly open at the top. Does he represent yet another of the Seven Deadly Sins, Avarice?

Centre

The background is of trees and foliage. A large owl stands in the middle looking to the front. On the branches are many smaller birds with their heads turned to the owl. The far wing of the owl is half unfurled. Owls form a popular subject for the carvers of misericords. Three owls, each carved with distinction, appear among the Norwich Cathedral misericords. Owls appear among misericords in many other places including Beverley Minster, Ely and Gloucester Cathedrals. The owl, as derived from medieval bestiaries, becomes a symbol of the Jews who, when offered the faith of Christ, chose darkness rather than light. The 'mobbing' of the owl by the smaller birds represents a constant challenge to the owl's position.

Supporters

Left and Right: a crested bird stands each side, set in a circular stem.

Elbow-rests

Left: As for N16 Right.

Right: A page wears a plumed head-dress, a short tunic, parted at the chest and scalloped at the hem. He holds a shield bearing the arms of Norwich Priory: silver a cross sable.

Centre

A fat man holding a tankard sits on a careering sow. The carving clearly portrays Gluttony, one of the Seven Deadly Sins. Trees are in the background to the right. The sow appears to be moving at some pace. Its legs are in motion, its head is lifted up, and the man is losing his hat off the back of his head. The sow's ridged back, curled tail, and array of udders are evident. Gluttony's balding head is tipped back. He clutches a large tankard with his left hand on the handle, and his right hand is at its base. But he is tipping the drink not into his mouth but under his chin, and the carver has secured the effect of the liquor spilling down the outside of his throat and down his tunic. His portliness is emphasized by the thin belt round his tunic which is skirted below the waist. A small scrip is attached to the belt. Gluttony has boots, turned down just below the knees, which have long turned-up toes. By his belly is an empty bowl, apparently attached to him by strings. Above the sow's head is a jug of ale. The picture given is one of unlicensed depravity. Perhaps nowhere in medieval literature is Gluttony more vividly described than in Passus VII of Langland's *Piers Plowman* when Gluttony visits the nearby tavern and behaves in a bestial fashion. His girth is likened to that of two greedy sows: 'Hus guttes gonne godely as two gredy sowes'. (17)

Supporters

Left and Right: On each side is a merman with a spiralled club held over the shoulder. With the other hand each holds the end of his tail. From the waist downwards the mermen have scaled bodies and a curled bifurcated fish tail. At the waist their tunics terminate, on the left with a scroll effect, and on the right with circular medallions. Their faces are beaked and turned inwards and upwards. They, like their feminine counterparts, are agents of beguilement.

Elbow-rests

Left: As for N17 Right.

Right: A patriarch with beard and flowing, scalloped cowl.

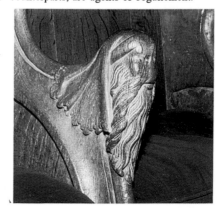

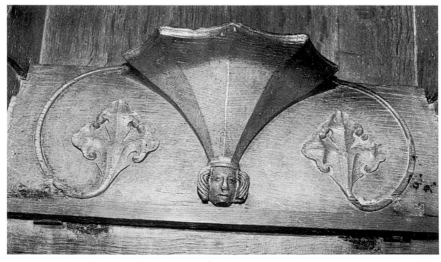

Centre

The six concave sides of the misericord seat are supported by a corbel comprising the head of a young man. He is wearing a fillet from under which his hair waves out on either side of his face. The face is small. This form of misericord is unique in Norwich Cathedral.

Supporters

Left and Right: Formal foliage.

Elbow-rests

Left: As for N18 Right.

Right: An old bearded man with a swept back cap. He wears breast, shoulder and elbow armour and gauntlets of which only the cuff is showing, as the rest is in the mouth of a wide-jawed monster. It has large pointed ears, its eyes are open, and it grips its victim between two sets of teeth. The old man is in the mouth of hell. A number of bench-ends in St Germaine's Wiggenhall, Norfolk, depict the perpetrators of the Seven Deadly Sins being trapped within the jaws of hell.

Centre

The curved moulding of the ledge indicates that this misericord was carved in the 1480s, and it is probable that the bishop represented is Bishop James Goldwell, 1472-1499. The bishop's mitre has the appearance of being squashed sideways by the pressure of the ledge from above. The mitre is decorated by a beading along its edges and down the middle. A floral pattern, perhaps of Tudor roses, is set beneath each of the two horns. The bishop's hair is swept back from beneath his mitre. His beard is parted in the middle of his chin and curled on either side in formal segments. The face might well represent a realistic portrait of Bishop Goldwell.

Supporters

Each supporter is of a dove in flight, with wings spread, tail upright, emerging from a nest of clouds.

Elbow-rests

Left: A capped figure supporting a shield. He wears a long tunic with swept back sleeves. His shoes are pointed. His features are worn smooth with age.

Right: A peasant with a protruding chest in a short-skirted tunic, and pointed shoes. He is holding his buttocks with both hands.

Centre

An angel emerges from the clouds. His wings are partially extended. He wears a fillet around his hair. On his shoulders is a scapular beneath which is a pleated gown. He holds up his left hand. His right hand clasps the wide girdle at his waist.

Supporters

Each side is a circular leaf the tips of which curl backwards on to the leaf.

Elbow-rests

Left: As for N20 Right.

Right: A shield-bearer wearing a long gown. He wears a head-dress, swept back sleeves and pointed shoes, turned inwards to each other. On the shield are crossed weapons: one resembles a lance and the other a cudgel.

Centre

A calf, with a tail with a curly end which is twisted over its back, has its head thrust up beneath the ledge. Its mouth is open. It wears a collar round its neck. Its rear feet have hooves and its fore-feet paws.

Supporters

The ledge has been damaged and there are no supporters.

Elbow-rests

Left: as for N21 Right.

Right: A man in a long gown with a girdle at the waist. The folds of his head-dress, the wings of his elbows, and the sleeve-ends that extend to the full length of his gown, are carved in detail on either side. His hands rest on his knees.

Centre

A lion lies in the centre. Its mane curls over its breast and sets in waves above its forehead. The face of the lion is turned to the front and its mouth is open revealing the teeth. The lion's tail twists away extravagantly to the right and sweeps up to the underside of the ledge. On the left of the lion a fierce, ring-necked, wyvern appears to be biting the lion's ear. The carving probably depicts the impact of evil on good. The medieval romance of Yvain tells of a lion unable to escape from a serpent which holds it by its tail. Yvain intervenes to rescue the lion. (18)

Supporters

Each side is a five-petalled rose.

Elbow-rests

Left: As for N22 Right.

Right: A fully clad figure with a pendent head-dress, in the mouth of a bat-eared, wide-eyed monster.

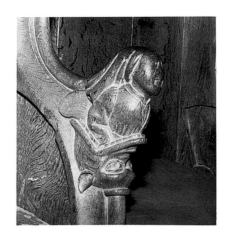

N24

Centre

A Green Man. Leaves curl from either side of his mouth, and from between his brows. Pomegranate-like fruit grows from this foliage by his ears and in the middle of his forehead. The face is large and forbidding and made more menacing by the showing of the teeth and the cross-eyed stare.

Supporters

Left and Right are foliate forms on a rose petal base.

Elbow-rests

Left: As for N23 Right.

Right: A bearded man, bald-headed in front, but with curly hair at the back. He has puffed shoulders with full sleeves. He holds in both hands, between his knees, a long jug, which has a handle on the left side.

Centre

A wyvern with head turned round on to its body. Its mouth is open and its tongue dangles out to one side. It has a horn in its head. Its body is scaly and the crest of its head and the ridge of its back are beaded. Its segmented tail curves up to beneath the ledge.

Supporters

Left: Missing.
Right: A fan of foliage.

Elbow-rests

Left: As for N24 Right.

Right: A mainly bald-headed man who has a little curly hair at the back of his head. His sleeves are puffed at the shoulders. He is caught between the jaws of a monster. He holds on with both hands to the monster's teeth.

Centre

A fortified town. It is surrounded by a castellated wall with a turret surmounted by a spire at the extremities left and right. In the front are strong double gates above which is a raised portcullis. The gate on the right stands slightly open. Within the town is the keep of a castle. Trees are seen within the walls on either side. The Common Seal of the city of Norwich made in 1404, showing the walls of a fortified city with a large central keep, has many similar features the most significant being a raised portcullis making access to the city available. (10)

Supporters

On either side a fan of foliage.

Elbow-rests

Left: As for N25 Right.

Right: An old man with long hair curled upwards. He is bearded. His hat flows back from a wide rolled brim. He wears a long gown. He clutches a bag of money in front of him. It is tied at the top by a cord on which the man has placed both hands. There are patterned bands round his upper arms. He represents the Deadly Sin of Avarice.

Centre

On the right an ape-like devil pushes a wheel-barrow. His left arm is broken. The wheel-barrow handle on the left side is also broken. In the wheel-barrow, with one leg in and one leg out, is another ape. He is holding with both hands, (the right arm has broken off), a bundle of birch twigs, bound together at the base by two bands. He seems to be striking the face of the other ape who has his face twisted to one side as though to avoid the full force of the blow. On the left yet another ape is standing with his right hand on the wheel of the wheel-barrow. Three trees stand in the background. Whittingham comments that the hopping ape is a symbol of lust.

Supporters

Left and Right: On either side, within the curved rib that stems from the ledge, is a wyvern with curled tail, extended cusped wing, but with a human face and long curly hair.

Elbow-rests

Left: As for N26 Right.

Right: A bearded man wearing a hat with a rolled brim. His mouth is open showing his teeth. His face is contorted and his whole expression is one of anguish. He has puffed shoulders to his sleeves. He is in the mouth of a monster.

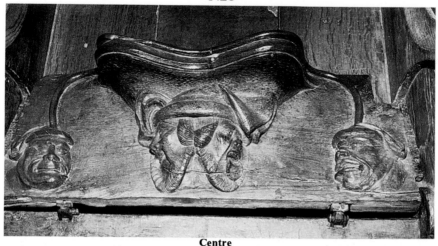

Centre

Two heads, set on one neck, look in opposite directions. The heads share the same hat which comprises a rolled brim over which decorative folds of cloth appear above each forehead. Curly hair and a fringed beard are on both faces. The head on the left is of a firm handsome countenance with a closed mouth. The one on the right shows his tongue, which is hanging a long way out of his mouth, and his teeth. His mouth is wide open and he appears to be shouting. The carving must represent an image of deceit or double-dealing. The Roman god Janus, after whom the month January is named, is sometimes portrayed with two faces, looking in opposite directions, on one neck, as though one face looks to the old year and one to the new. The Norwich carver may have had this classical image in mind. Two faces are represented under the same hood on a misericord at Worle in Somerset.(1)

Supporters

Left: A fat face looking towards the centre with a menacing grimace. He wears a hat. His teeth are clenched.

Right: A coarse face with thick lips, parted to show the teeth. The head is set on a bull-like neck. The face looks towards the centre. All hats carved in this misericord are of the rolled brim kind. In the Supporters the brims are patterned.

Elbow-rests

Left: As for N27 Right.

Right: An elderly man, bearded, wearing a long hat is in the mouth of a monster which has four beads set vertically on its forehead. The man's sleeves are puffed at the shoulders. His right hand is in the monster's mouth; his left hand is clearly shown.

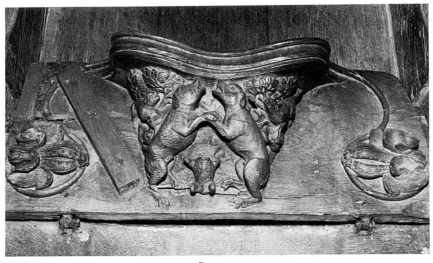

Centre

Two dogs are fighting each other standing on their hind legs. Their mouths are open, their jowls are turned upwards, and they appear to be barking. A smaller dog is carved either side of them. These emerge from a background of foliage. A damaged small figure, perhaps that of a monkey, with two arms and two legs broken off, is sitting beneath and between the fighting dogs. Its broken limbs are held out in front of it.

Supporters

On either side a pomegranate, placed horizontally and emerging from its leaves, points towards the centre.

Elbow-rests

Left: As for N28 Right.

Right: A page wearing a dagged tunic with puffed shoulders. He has long hair but no hat. His boots are banded below the knee. He holds in front of him a shield which bears no markings.

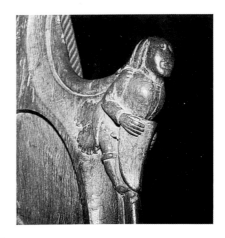

Centre

A man's figure emerges from a whorled shell. His head is cowled and he wears a scapular over his shoulders. His tunic is buttoned. In his right hand he holds a short sword. In his left hand he holds a small saddle, of which the middle part, which would rest on the horse's back, has been left uncarved. Whittingham believes the carving to represent a pilgrim. The shell and the saddle support this view more strongly than the brandished sword. (9)

Supporters

On either side is a ferocious monster with a large head, squashed ears, and open threatening mouth. By comparison its body is small. But it has a prominent tail that divides at the end into three wavy parts.

Elbow-rests

Left: A finely carved head of a young man. His forehead is high and wide. His hair curls either side of his face.

Right: An old man, bearded, writing at his desk which has been damaged. The man's head is cowled and his arms are missing.

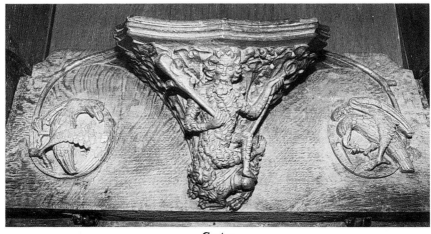

Centre
A wild man carries a knobbly club in his right hand and a rope with a loop at the end in his left hand. The other end of the rope is tied around the neck of a lion which the wild man has subdued. Indeed he is sitting cross-legged on top of the lion. The wild man has on his head an abundance of wavy hair and also a long curly beard. His body is entirely covered with matted hair. Behind his head are oak leaves and acorns. (9)

Supporters
Left: In a circular carving, taking its shape from the curved rib coming from the ledge, an eagle bends back its head and neck to preen its extended wing.
Right: This also is circular in design. An eagle with its wings folded above seems to be holding some food in its right talons and pecks at it with its hooked beak.

Elbow-rests

Left: The hatless head of a man with large ears, prominent neck, and beard parted in the middle. The grain of the wood adds considerable interest to the face.
Right: A tumbler bending over backwards. This is a beautifully conceived carving. Different woods have been used, perhaps in the course of repair, but it gives the effect of the tumbler having a parti-coloured costume and hose. The tumbler is a young man with his hair thrown back. He holds his shins. He wears a round-necked tunic and a medallioned belt with scrip attached. His shoes have ankle straps, like a type of ballet shoe. The carving in this stall has been undertaken by a master craftsman.

Book List

1. Anderson, M.D. *The Medieval Carver,* Cambridge 1935 (p.40).
2. Anderson, M.D. *Drama and Imagery in English Medieval Churches,* Cambridge 1963.
3. Anderson, M.D. *History and Imagery in British Churches,* Edinburgh 1971.
4. Anderson, M.D. *Lincoln Choir-Stalls,* Lincoln 1951 and 1967.
5. Bond, F. *Misericords,* Oxford 1910 (p.103-5).
6. Bourchier, Sir John, trans. *The Chronicles of Froissart,* 1901-3 (p.97-8).
7. Dorling, E.E. *Medieval Heraldry Remaining in the Cathedral Church of Norwich,* Norwich 1933 (p.17-20).
8. Goulburn, E.M. *Ancient Sculptures in the Roof of Norwich Cathedral,* London 1876 (p.442 & 447).
9. Hart, R. *Misereres,* Norfolk & Norwich Archaeological Society Vol. II, 1849, (p.246)
10. Hudson, W. & Tingey, J., *Records of the City of Norwich Vol. II,* Norwich 1911 (p. 278).
11. Jancey, M. *Mappa Mundi,* Hereford 1987.
12. Laird, M. *English Misericords,* London 1986 (pl.44 & 120).
13. Remnant, G.L. *Catalogue of Misericords in Great Britain,* Oxford 1969.
14. Remnant, Mary *English Bowed Instruments from Anglo-Saxon to Tudor Times,* Oxford 1986.
15. Repton, J.A. *Norwich Cathedral,* Farnborough, Hants. 1965 (p.6).
16. Rubin, Miri, *Corpus Christi,* Cambridge 1992, (p.310-2).
17. Skeat, W.W., ed. *Piers the Plowman,* London 1873 (Passus VII 1.398, Passus VIII 1. 105-7).
18. Stevens, John *Medieval Romance,* London 1973 (p.72).
19. Tracy, C. *English Gothic Choir-Stalls 1200-1400,* Bury St Edmunds 1987 (p.4 & 37, pl. 181).
20. Tracy, C. *Englsh Gothic Choir-Stalls 1400-1540,* Bury St Edmunds 1990.
21. Truax, Elizabeth *Metamorphosis in Shakespeare's Plays,*New York 1992, (p.88)
22. White, T.H. *The Book of Beasts being a translation from a Latin Bestiary of the Twelfth Century,* London 1954 (p.132-3).
23. Whittingham, A.B.*The Stalls of Norwich Cathedral,* Norwich 1948 (p.12 & 15).
24. Whittingham, A.B. *Norwich Cathedral Bosses and Misericords,* Norwich 1981.

Arthur Whittingham in his two publications on the cathedral's misericords has provided an excellent record of the complicated history of the choir-stalls, together with a brief description of the misericord carvings. The thoroughness of his historical research has been warmly endorsed by Charles Tracy, the author of a more recent work which dealt with the development of choir-stalls throughout the country. This present study owes an immeasurable debt to Whittingham. It aims however to illustrate all the misericords and to give a full description of each, which was not possible within the scope of Whittingham's 1948 and 1981 publications. But this present work does not pretend to give a detailed account of the choir-stalls, a subject admirably covered by both Whittingham and Tracy.